THE WORLD OF AUTOMOBILES

Carmakers from Around the Globe

Written by Norm Geddis

The World of Automobiles

Carmakers from Around the Globe

Concept Cars: Past and Future

Customizing Your Ride

Hop Inside the Most Exotic Cars

Toughest Trucks from the Streets to Showtime

THE WORLD OF AUTOMOBILES

Carmakers from Around the Globe

Written by Norm Geddis

MC

MASON CREST

Mason Crest
450 Parkway Drive, Suite D
Broomall, Pennsylvania 19008
(866) MCP-BOOK (toll free)

First printing
9 8 7 6 5 4 3 2 1

ISBN (hardback) 978-1-4222-4087-8
ISBN (series) 978-1-4222-4086-1
ISBN (ebook) 978-1-4222-7706-5

Library of Congress Cataloging-in-Publication Data

Names: Geddis, Norm, author.
Title: Carmakers from around the globe / Norm Geddis.
Description: Broomall, Pennsylvania : Mason Crest, [2019] | Series: The world of automobiles | Includes bibliographical references and index.
Identifiers: LCCN 2018018045 (print) | LCCN 2018019229 (ebook) | ISBN 9781422277065 (eBook) | ISBN 9781422240878 (hardback) | ISBN 9781422240861(series)
Subjects: LCSH: Automobile--Technological innovations--Juvenile literature. | Automobile industry and trade--Juvenile literature.
Classification: LCC TL147 (ebook) | LCC TL147 .G43 2019 (print) | DDC 338.7/629222--dc23
LC record available at https://lccn.loc.gov/2018018045

Developed and Produced by National Highlights Inc.
Editor: Andrew Luke
Interior and cover design: Annalisa Gumbrecht, Studio Gumbrecht
Production: Michelle Luke

QR CODES AND LINKS TO THIRD-PARTY CONTENT

CONTENTS

KEY ICONS TO LOOK FOR:

Words to understand: These words with their easy-to-understand definitions will increase the reader's understanding of the text while building vocabulary skills.

Sidebars: This boxed material within the main text allows readers to build knowledge, gain insights, explore possibilities, and broaden their perspectives by weaving together additional information to provide realistic and holistic perspectives.

Educational videos: Readers can view videos by scanning our QR codes, providing them with additional educational content to supplement the text. Examples include news coverage, moments in history, speeches, iconic sports moments, and much more!

Text-dependent questions: These questions send the reader back to the text for more careful attention to the evidence presented there.

Research projects: Readers are pointed toward areas of further inquiry connected to each chapter. Suggestions are provided for projects that encourage deeper research and analysis.

Series of glossary of key terms: This back-of-the-book glossary contains terminology used throughout this series. Words found here increase the reader's ability to read and comprehend higher-level books and articles in this field.

CEO
stands for Chief Executive Officer, the person who is sthe leader of a company

merger
any combination of two or more business enterprises into a single enterprise

postwar
of, relating to, or characteristic of a period following World War II

CHAPTER 1

Introduction

Riding down the freeway, the world appears to be full of Fords, Nissans, Toyotas, Mercedes, Hondas, and a handful of Volvos and Subarus, with a Ferrari roaring by now and then. Turn off at a row of car dealerships and the lots are full of bright and colorful cars waiting for new owners. Some of the cars on those lots come from factories close by, other come from the other side of the world. In fact, around the world there exist many more carmakers than those that make the models that shows up on local roads. China has around two

Car dealership lots can be full of cars made in nearby factories or in countries thousands of miles away.

dozen carmakers, but few of its cars are exported out of that country.

Today, the United States has what are called the Big Three automakers, though one of those three is now primarily a European company. The Big Three are Ford, GM, and Fiat-Chrysler. But the United States once had many more companies—several hundred, in fact, over the course of the last 130 years or so.

Even when car companies make a successful car, their longevity isn't guaranteed. The same strengths of its managers and workers that helped the company come into existence and take off—things like imagination, ingenuity, and determination—can also result in unwillingness to compromise.

Several automotive entrepreneurs have been forward thinking geniuses. Several have been stubborn to the point of hurting the companies they ran. The car-making business is tough. Today in the United States, the Big Three are the only companies still around out of hundreds that existed at the time of the Great Depression.

In the later years of the twentieth century, several of those small car companies struggled to continue. In a complicated series of purchases and **mergers**, they showed that even though a car manufacturer may have billions of dollars in the bank and an infrastructure of factories around the country, profits can be elusive, and a business can only lose money for so long.

After World War II, the Big Three automakers—Ford, GM, and Chrysler—were developing innovative distribution and financing systems that helped them sell cars for lower prices. This innovation drove the smaller automakers into a long and slow decline. Through the 1950s, the companies of Nash-

Kelvinator, the Hudson Motor Car Company, Studebaker, and Packard all suffered continually declining sales.

The original idea for American Motors Corporation was a merger of all four of these smaller companies into a single entity that could compete on all levels with the Big Three. However, an old business rivalry prevented the larger merger from happening.

George W. Mason, the head of Nash motors, was the mastermind behind the new American Motors Corporation, which instead consisted of just the Nash and Hudson companies. He was the company's first **CEO**.

World War II had given all of America's car companies work building trucks, tanks, boats, and any other kind of military

The Hornet, like this 1954 edition, is a famous model from Hudson, one of the companies that would form the American Motors Corporation.

equipment using steel and wheels. These were by and large also the companies that made the motors, chassis, transmissions, axles, and every other vehicle component. In the **postwar** economic boom, all these companies returned to making their money by building things for and selling things to consumers.

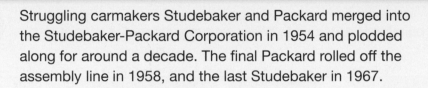

END OF THE LINE

Struggling carmakers Studebaker and Packard merged into the Studebaker-Packard Corporation in 1954 and plodded along for around a decade. The final Packard rolled off the assembly line in 1958, and the last Studebaker in 1967.

Watch as the last Studebakers come off the assembly line in Hamilton, ON, in 1966.

Although historically considered one of the ugliest cars ever made, the Gremlin, like this 1973 model, was a popular AMC creation.

AMC found a place in the car market by building small, inexpensive, and fuel-efficient vehicles more than a decade before fuel shortages motivated the development of fuel-efficient cars by the Big Three. The AMC Rambler and Gremlin were the company's most successful car models, though sales lagged behind AMC's next acquisition.

American Motors Corporation added one more independent automaker in 1970, the last US independent automaker with a star product: the Jeep. The Jeep, which had been designed and built for the US Military by Kaiser Motors in World War II, was the company's only line of vehicles. They were popular, but with such a small operation, Kaiser was not able to make much of profit. So, they joined forces with AMC, and the Jeep turns out to be the only AMC product still being made today, though by Fiat-Chrysler.

AMC had their own troubles by the mid-1980s that led to the company being acquired by Chrysler, but the problems weren't so much to do with poor sales. The Jeep was more popular than ever. Gasoline in the United States was fairly cheap, and people were starting to purchase bigger cars. The newest player in the American car game couldn't keep up.

AMC's troubles were due to a perfect storm of technical and management problems. The company had trouble getting ideas from the drawing board to the assembly line. They had aging plants that had not been updated since the Nash days. The company procedures for re-tooling a factory were time consuming and outdated. So, while the Jeep was selling great, AMC's vast compact car line was floundering.

Under the control of AMC, which acquired Jeep in 1970, Jeep made models like this 1980 Jeep Scrambler.

A previous and unrelated American Motors Corporation existed between the years 1920 and 1924. Ironically, Louis Chevrolet, one of the founders of Chevrolet motors, headed this company. This American Motors Corporation made cars in New Jersey and, through a series of mergers with numerous companies, ended up a part of a company called Amalgamated Motors. Amalgamated Motors has been lost to history. It is unknown if they ever made a single car. The only remains of Amalgamated Motors are stock certificates that sell among collectors for around $80.

Other countries also saw the rise and fall of well-known brands. In Sweden, postwar carmaker Saab rolled its first automobile model, the Saab 92, off the line in 1949. The company produced more than a million cars over the next

This 1983 Saab 900 GLE is one of a million 900s the Swedish carmaker produced between 1978 and 1998.

thirty years. From 1978 to 1998, the company produced nearly a million of its classic Saab 900 model. At the turn of the century, however, Saab (which had been purchased by GM) began to flounder, as it could not compete with high-volume luxury models like Audi and BMW but could not command the price point of fellow low-volume producers like Porsche. The company went out of business in 2011.

In England, Triumph started out as a brand that built big luxury cars in the 1920s and 1930s. Those cars did not sell well, however, and Standard Motor Company bought Triumph in the 1940s and reinvented it as the sports car brand it is historically remembered as. By the 1960s, however, quality and reliability issues caused sales to decline, and Triumph eventually folded in 1984.

The TR6 is one of the best-selling Triumph models. They were made between 1968 and 1976, like this 1972 version.

The pages of automotive history are spattered with the remains of companies that have imploded and collapsed for a variety of reasons. Yet, as in any industry, the success stories of the strong companies persist, and in the upcoming chapters, we will travel around the globe to tell them.

 ## TEXT-DEPENDENT QUESTIONS

1. True or False? All three of America's Big Three automakers are own by purely American interests.
2. What two companies formed the American Motors Corporation?
3. Which country did Saabs come from?

RESEARCH PROJECT

This chapter mentioned failed carmakers like Packard and Studebaker, but there are many others that tried to make the next great American automobile. Research and find two others that lasted at least 10 years and write a brief report on each, including pictures of the models they produced.

dealership
a business, usually not affiliated with the manufacturer, which buys, stocks and sells automobiles

voting stock
a financial instrument that when purchased gives the buyer a vote on certain company decisions

multi-national
a term used for companies that have business headquarters in two or more countries

CHAPTER 2

United States

The United States has grown one of the largest native auto industries in the world. However, only two of its oldest makers, General Motors and Ford, are still majority owned by US entities. Also, a large state Chinese company has a sizeable investment in GM. That said, US automakers are truly international. Almost all major car markets have not only US automaker dealerships, but factories as well, with some of them making cars that are essentially native to the country where they are made, like Ford's Troller brand in South America.

General Motors has been building cars in the United States since 1908, but has its roots in Buick, which produced its first car in 1899.

Several new companies are threatening to break into the US market, and one of them, Tesla, has already taken market share from the other American makers. While the American business landscape is littered with hundreds of defunct automakers, today there are essentially the two from old days (Fiat-Chrysler is now a European company) and two in their infancy, and one, Tesla, in the toddler stage.

General Motors

It is hard to come up with a good adjective to describe GM at the moment, but weird might be the one. GM does make some of the world's most renowned cars. GM is also simultaneously one of the world's newest and one of the world's oldest automobile companies. During the Global Economic Crisis of 2008, General Motors, one of America's oldest car companies, was close to closing its factories and going out of business.

GM nearly went bankrupt during the Global Economic Crisis of 2008, but the US government bailed the company out.

That did not happen in spite of the fact that General Motors could not pay its debts. The US government loaned GM enough money to keep the company in business. As an employer of more than 200,000 individuals, the US government felt that those employees and the world economy, as a whole, were deserving of a special effort to give General Motors a new chance to keep making and selling cars.

By taking advantage of a US government program called The Troubled Asset Relief Program, GM reorganized itself into a new business in 2009.

The original company was founded by William C. Durant on September 16, 1908. Durant was a straight-forward and uninspiring industrialist, not nearly as forward-thinking and charismatic as Henry Ford. He made his fortune manufacturing and selling horse-drawn carriages. In fact, his horse-drawn carriage company, the Durant-Dort Carriage Company, was the largest carriage maker in the United States at the turn of the twentieth century.

He also made a good income from several Ford **dealerships** he owned. In a sense, Ford helped bring GM into existence. Durant himself believed the automobile to be impractical and dangerous. When he decided to go into the car-making business, he put his fortune into a holding company called General Motors. He then used GM to purchase already existing automobile companies. The goal of General Motors was to make a safer car.

The first purchase was Buick, and soon after Cadillac and Oldsmobile were brought under the GM umbrella. Dozens of carmakers ended up being bought by GM, and many of the names have been forgotten, like Rapid Motors, for example. Another example is Oakland, which became the Pontiac brand, one-time producer of GM's top line of mid- and full-size family cars in the

1970s. Pontiac lost its footing in the market at the turn of the century and declining sales led to GM shuttering the brand in 2010.

Today GM makes cars all over the world, with a large presence in the United States, China, and Brazil. In the United States, the brands GM sells are Chevrolet, Buick, GMC, and Cadillac. Popular models include the Chevrolet Cruze, Silverado, Equinox, and Malibu, as well as the GMC Sierra. GM, like other big car companies, sees its future in providing more than cars for the individual. They are developing transportation systems using artificial intelligence, self-driving cars, and ride-sharing concepts.

The Chevy Cruze is one of the best-selling current GM models.

William C. Durant, the founder of General Motors, made part of his early fortune by owning several Ford car dealerships. He also owned a company that made spring components for Ford. Durant's name is not as well-known as Ford's because, first, he did not have a reputation as a showman like Ford, and second, he never stayed in one place for very long. Soon after founding General Motors he was forced out of the company by stockholders. He then helped found Chrysler. After that, he regained control of General Motors for a few years before being forced out again. Durant Motors was his next enterprise, which despite a semi-successful line of cars, could not manage to survive the Great Depression. Here Durant's story takes a dark turn. After a small stroke in 1942 left him partially paralyzed, he took a job managing a bowling alley in Flint, MI. His whereabouts in the months before his death are largely unknown, but William C. Durant was found dead in New York City in 1942.

Ford

Ford is a **multi-national** carmaker that remains, in essence, a family business. Founded by Henry Ford in 1903, the corporation has always had at least one Ford in a top position within the company. The family retains 40% of the company's **voting stock**, far more than stockholders in any other automobile entity. This pretty much gives the family final say over what happens at Ford.

Ford operates two brands beside their own "Ford" marque. They make the Lincoln and Troller brands of vehicles. Troller makes one vehicle for the Brazilian off-road market, the T4.

The Ford family still retains 40% of the company, which is headquartered in the Detroit suburb of Dearborn, MI.

This is a popular Jeep-styled vehicle that has proven itself capable of driving on almost any surface in almost any condition. Brazil's largest city, São Paulo, suffered a wide and deep flood in 2009. During this time, the T4 made news as it crossed the flooded city on live television, showing that the T4 was a vehicle for the most rugged situations.

The Lincoln brand is Ford's luxury line that has seen some major changes in the last few years. While known for big cars like the Town Car and Mark VIII, Lincoln shed the last of those models in 2012 to concentrate on a new line of sedans, SUVs, and crossovers. The MKC crossover is Lincoln's most popular vehicle today. The 6-speed automatic transmission on the MKC is operated from the entertainment system through a set of virtual buttons, hearkening back to 1950s push-button transmissions.

Lincoln is Ford's luxury brand, making models like the MKZ, MKC, and MKT.

Ford currently makes twenty car models and eight truck/van models for the North American, South American, and European markets. The Ka model, a smaller version of the Fiesta, is popular in Brazil. The B, C, and S series are similar cars for the European market. Ford's current sports car, the second-generation GT, premiered at the 2015 North American Auto Show. The car goes from 0 to 60 mph (0 to 97 km/h) in under three seconds with a top speed of 216 mph (348 km/h).

Ford has recently announced a commitment to refocus car manufacturing on fully electric cars by investing $11 billion in research and development. Ford makes only one electric car as of 2018, a variant of its Focus compact car that manages only about one hundred miles on a full charge, which pales in comparison to Tesla's models. Ford created an all-electric version of its Ranger pickup truck in the early 2000s. The truck was made available only for industry use, though some private individuals were able to lease them.

The future of Ford looks to be in creating self-driving electric vehicles. Though the company is currently behind in development of this technology, they are promising big things, including the all-electric Mach 1 and fully autonomous vehicles in 2020 or 2021.

Watch a 1926 promotional movie for a Ford Model T truck.

Best known for computers and mobile communication devices, Apple may be delving into car making in the near future.

Apple?

Will Apple make an electric car? Who knows. But if they don't make some kind of firm announcement soon, they may find that when they do, nobody cares. Strange-looking cars have been seen on the road around a semisecret Apple testing facility.

Apple is being very tight lipped about what they are doing. The company has been hiring hundreds of engineers with backgrounds in automobiles and autonomous driving. They have said that they are working on systems related to autonomous driving but have given no firm indication they intend to build an actual car.

Since flirting with becoming the first trillion-dollar company in the world, Apple has the money and status to break into car making, though they may see a better future in providing technology to other manufacturers.

NIKOLA TESLA

Tesla is named after the famous and mysterious physicist Nikola Tesla. Any college engineering student will typically have at least one Nikola Tesla t-shirt. This is because the man was reported to have accomplished some strange things with electricity, including lighting up a town from a distance without wires and talking to people on other planets. While some of his "wireless electricity" experiments produced interesting results, it turns out that his communication with other planets was him receiving the first Morse Code transmissions through his lab equipment.

Tesla

What other company has a car racing through space? Elon Musk, the driving force behind Tesla, launched a cherry red Roadster from his company's SpaceX rocket in 2018. Tesla knows how to put on a good show but bringing an affordable electric car to the masses

The launch of Musk's SpaceX Falcon 9 from Lompoc, CA in 2017.

is proving a difficult task. Car journalists are questioning whether the company's Model 3 can fill the space in the market it intends to fill. The Model 3 is looking to be the Ford Taurus of the twenty-first century, that affordable car with innovative design and technology that always seems to appear at the end of an economic recession. However, with more than two hundred thousand back orders and only a few hundred produced at the end of 2017, Tesla's race to the future appears to have been stalled by the problems of the present.

Elon Musk's Tesla Inc. has had impressive success selling its electric-powered vehicles.

Tesla is the world's first all-electric car company since the early twentieth century. Two engineers who were frustrated that the all-electric EV-1 model from GM had been taken off the market founded the company in 2003.

The original founders soon got the attention of famous entrepreneur Elon Musk, who put over $7 million of his own money into the company. They have successfully produced, marketed, and sold three models, with the Model 3 in problematic initial production and a new Roadster on the way . . . well, one new Roadster in particular is on its way to Mars or the asteroid belt. The new Roadster will be available to the rest of us in 2020, according to Tesla.

Tesla sales have grown at a rate unseen by any car company that is "new" in the sense that it never in any way existed before its birthday. Companies like GM and Chrysler have reorganized in recent years and are technically "new" companies, but those companies have predecessors of the same name with the same primary people working for them. After less than two decades in existence, Tesla went from nothing to selling more than 250,000 units in 2017.

Plus, these have been sales of electric cars. Pick any decade since early electric cars disappeared, and it will not be hard to find a start-up looking to revolutionize the car industry with an electric car. All of them failed. Whatever Tesla's future, they already have made an auto-industry breakthrough not seen since the early days of car manufacturing.

Global sales of Tesla's Model S have topped two hundred thousand units.

Tesla's Model 3 back order problem is reminiscent of the problems faced by another once-high-flying innovative car company. The last steam-powered car was the Doble Model E. Abner Doble was a true believer in steam power, but a poor business person. He bankrupted several of his previous companies on his way to the Model E. Though an amazing car (most of the fifty that were made are still on the road today), Doble had soured his reputation in the business world and could not secure the credit he needed to produce the Model E, even though he had more than five thousand pre-orders. The last Doble was made in 1931.

Telsa's export sales have been strong with more than $1 billion in sales in China. Along with additional "gigafactories" going up in the United States, Tesla will also build a factory in Shanghai.

The first Tesla was the Model S, the first of which went to its owner in June of 2012. The Model S can go around 325 miles on a single charge.

The next model was the Model X, a full-size crossover SUV that was released in 2015. Though delivery of the Model X had been delayed several times, by the time the first one rolled off the assembly line, Tesla had thirty thousand pre-orders for the vehicle.

The Model S and the Model X are both aimed at the luxury car market and affluent buyers. Tesla has aimed its next model at everyone. The Model 3 competes with mid-size cars in the $30,000 price range, making it accessible to the average car buyer. Tesla has received five hundred thousand reservations for purchases of a Model 3 since July of 2017. However, setbacks in production have meant that less than two thousand have been made through the end of 2017.

No car has had a pre-order success like the Model 3. The closest might be Citroen which received one hundred thousand pre-orders at a car show in Paris in the 1950s. Tesla's future now depends not on it making an electric car succeed—they've done that—but on keeping the company from floundering by getting Model 3s into customers' garages.

Waymo

Waymo is Alphabet's self-driving car company. Alphabet Inc. is the parent company of Google. Before Alphabet set up Waymo and announced details about their car's development, the car was referred to in press rumors as "the Google car."

No date has been given for the release of a car, nor has any concept car been displayed. Cars using Google self-driving technology have been in on the road in northern California in recent years, but these cars have been modified versions of different retail

Waymo is the self-driving car company from the parent company of Google.

cars. Waymo recently agreed to buy several thousand minivans from Fiat-Chrysler.

Waymo has been using their self-driving technology in Fiat-Chrysler minivans and Lexus SUVs for a few years. They have road-tested their self-driving technology more than any other company in their field. Their cars saw more than 126,000 miles of autonomous driving in 2016. In 2017, the number exceeded 650,000 miles. Test vehicles also included a Prius and an Audi TT.

Whether Waymo will produce and market its own car remains to be seen. They are way ahead on the self-driving technology front, and like Apple, the company may feel a better fit in the market will be as a developer and driver of technology, but not a maker of cars.

TEXT-DEPENDENT QUESTIONS

1. What was the name of the founder of General Motors?
2. True or False? Tesla has completed production of 200,000 Model 3 cars.
3. Waymo is owned by what parent company?

RESEARCH PROJECT

Do some research on the popular companies Google and Apple. Use the facts you discover to explain which one of these non-traditional potential carmakers you would be more likely to buy a car from.

contractor
a person or company hired to perform work or to provide goods at a certain price or within a certain time

hybrid-powered
having two different types of components (gas and electric) performing the function of providing power to an engine

supermini
a car category in Europe and Japan that is defined as being bigger than a mini but smaller than a small family car; the subcompact car is the equivalent term in North America

CHAPTER 3

Japan

Toyota

The world's largest carmaker makes more than ten million cars a year and has been doing so since 2010. In less than a century, Toyota reached the status of the #1 carmaker in the world measured by the number of cars produced.

They have also managed to transform how cars are powered, something that forty years ago most auto industry executives would have laughed at. The **hybrid-powered** Prius line has been around for twenty years. While the car may at times be a punchline for a certain cartoon dog, love for the model is demonstrated by the fact that sales of Prius grew every year between the car's introduction in 1997 and 2010. Sales of the Prius are currently around 350,000 cars per year.

TOYODA

Toyota was originally spelled Toyoda, which is the true spelling of the founding family's name. The world Toyoda means "fertile rice paddies" in Japanese. Since the family didn't want their car company to be associated with old-fashioned farming equipment they changed the letter d to a t. The word "Toyota" requires eight brush strokes in simplified Japanese writing, a lucky number in the country's traditional culture.

Toyota grew out of the Toyoda Automatic Loom Works in the early 1930s. What are looms? They are a piece of machinery used to speed up the production of fabrics. Looms are still a part of Toyota's product line, though today's looms use computers and robotics. Toyota also makes sewing machines.

While Toyota produced cars beginning in 1937, large numbers of automobiles weren't produced until after World War II, beginning in 1947 with the introduction of the Toyopet. Made for purchase in Japan, the two-door sedan looked similar to the Volkswagen Beetle, though with a classier front end.

The first Toyota exported to the United States was the Crown in 1955, a luxury model still in production today. Be that as it may, the United States was not the first country in the Americas to get a Toyota. That distinction goes to the government of El Salvador, which purchased a dozen Toyota Land Cruisers a few years earlier in 1953.

The 1955 Crown was the first Toyota model to be exported to America.

Toyota sells about 350,000 of its hybrid model Prius around the world each year.

Today, Toyota makes more than seventy gas-powered models and thirty-four hybrid/electric models between the Toyota and Lexus brands. Among the best-selling car models are the Prius, Corolla, and Camry. The compact and mid-size markets are where Toyota dominates. Their Lexus luxury brand makes popular sedans and SUVs. Toyota operates worldwide across all levels of the vehicle market, making cars, trucks, and buses, both full-size and mini.

Honda

Honda has design facilities, research departments, and factories located all around the world. They are the world's eighth-largest carmaker, and the world's number one motorcycle producer. The company's assets are valued at more than $18 trillion. They also make watercraft, lawn equipment, and other motorized tools.

The company started as a **contractor** for Toyota, making piston rings. After World War II, like many Japanese industry start-ups, they made scooters from surplus war parts. The company first made motorcycles before it built and marketed its first production car in the early 1960s. The company quickly gained a reputation for high-quality engineering and workmanship.

Honda sells more than 1.5 million vehicles annually in the United States alone. They sell more than fifty brands worldwide. Like Toyota they concentrate on the mid-size market, with the Civic and Accord being the most popular models. Unlike Toyota, Honda makes its own supercar, the NSX. First made in the early 2000s, the NSX got a complete makeover in 2010 and stands today as the only supercar designed by a woman, Michelle Christensen.

H POWERED

Honda sees the future of automobile power to be in development of hydrogen fuel cells. To that end, the government of the State of California has agreed to spend close to $7 million for four H2 fueling stations. This represents the only current plan to build hydrogen fuel cell infrastructure in the United States.

The Honda NSX, seen here at the 2018 Brussels Motor Show in Belgium, is a supercar outside the compact- to mid-size sedan market typically serviced by Honda or Toyota.

Suzuki

Suzuki sold cars in the United States from the early 1980s until 2012. The exact date Suzuki entered the US market depends on how it's defined. Suzuki was making the Chevy Sprint for GM beginning in 1986. In fact, the popular Suzuki **supermini** model the Cultus was branded two ways in the United States, as the Geo Metro and Pontiac Firefly.

Watch the history of Subaru in about nine minutes, from 1954 to 2018.

The company entered the US auto market with its own brands at around the same time; they were already well known in the motorcycle market. While Suzuki left the US market in the early 2010s, they continue to make and sell more than two million cars worldwide each year. They recently entered the European mid- and full-size SUV market with the S4. They sell more than 80 percent of their cars in Europe. In the last few years, they have

Suzuki sells more than three million cars around the world each year, including the 2018 Swift Sport.

introduced several subcompact and supermini electric cars at shows around the world.

Mazda

Mazda began in the late-1920s as a machining company called Toyo Cork Kogyo making parts for other cars. In 1931, they produced their first vehicle—a motorized tricycle called the Mazda Go (its cars were always called Mazdas, even though that did not become the official company name until 1984).

Mazda made a point of focusing their engineering on developing a better Wankel rotary engine. The Wankel engine is a type of internal combustion engine that uses rotaries rather than pistons. This offers a couple of advantages over piston-driven engines. The engine offers equivalent power at one-third the size. The drawbacks are that it the Wankel takes longer to distribute speed and uses more fuel than a standard engine.

The Mazda CX5, like this 2018 model, is one of the company's popular crossover SUVs.

Mazda entered the US market in 1970, and Ford acquired 25% of the company in 1979, and shared production and engineering on joint projects across the two platforms, including Ford's Escort and Probe models and Mazda's Tribute compact SUV. Today Ford owns only about 2% of the company, and the joint projects have ended. Current Mazda models include the CX line of crossover SUVs and the Mazda 2, 3, and 6.

MOOZDA

Like many companies, Mazda seeks to be more environmentally friendly. They are currently making their car interiors out of 30% bio-material, using derivatives of milk and various types of cow byproducts.

TEXT-DEPENDENT QUESTIONS

1. True or False? Toyota began as a loom making company.

2. What type of alternative power does Honda see replacing gasoline-powered vehicles?

3. What type of engine is Mazda known for?

RESEARCH PROJECT

Japan is Asia's most established car making nation. China's track record in the industry is much shorter, but much like with everything else, the Chinese are catching up fast. Take a look at the Chinese auto industry and put together a chart that compares and contrasts the top five most popular models available there.

WORDS TO UNDERSTAND

air-cooled engine
an engine that is designed to be cooled by air-flow created by the car's forward-motion

robust
having or exhibiting strength or vigorous health

state-owned
a term similar to nationalization but where the company is and always has been owned by the government

CHAPTER 4

Germany

Germany stands out as having Europe's most **robust** and successful auto industry, sporting many of Europe's most elite automobiles. They have carmakers that produce cars with solid reputations across the entire scale of the automotive market. From inexpensive starter cars to elite supercars, German makers create more cars for fewer Euros than any other European company. For this reason, a Germany chapter is in order.

Volkswagen

Volkswagen is a German carmaker that makes more than ten million cars a year. They are one of the world's largest carmakers.

The classic Volkswagen Beetle was a popular first car for an entire generation of drivers in the 1970s.

In America, young people from the 1960s through the 1990s often had a Volkswagen as their first car. The Beetle is their most iconic car, but the Jetta, Passat, and the VW Bus also have long histories with mystiques all their own.

They have always been a car company focused on making an affordable car. Even so, the company's origins are just plain creepy, and their use of slave labor from German concentration camps was admittedly shameful.

Volkswagen began as the **state-owned** automaker under the control of the Nazi party's labor union. They spent the early 1930s developing a "people's car." This became the Volkswagen Beetle in later years.

After World War I, Germany had been restricted from bringing large amounts of steel into the county without a reason. The "people's car" served as their reason. Not many Nazi models of the "people's car" were made. One underhanded reason the German government had for developing a "people's car" was as a way of getting steel which could be diverted from making cars to making tanks, and other war weaponry, into the country.

After World War II, the company passed through the hands of the British military, which revived the company to make cars for use by occupying soldiers. Since VW re-established as an independent company, they have nothing but history in common with the original Nazi state-owned company.

Today they partner with automakers around the world in a large umbrella group dedicated to making affordable cars. Though Volkswagen got themselves in trouble in the last few years by lying about the effectiveness of their exhaust filters, they recently announced partnerships with Chinese companies to make alternatively powered cars. Today VW offers more than fifty models worldwide, including the Beetle, Golf, Jetta, Passat, and Tiguan.

The 2018 Tiguan is one of fifty models that VW offers worldwide.

Watch the restoration of a 1965 Volkswagen Beetle.

Audi

Audi is a German luxury carmaker that operates independently within the Volkswagen Group. 2018 marks the first year a car will be available with what is called "Level 3 Self Driving." That car is the Audi A8.

In terms of self-driving vehicles, Level 3 means that the driver is not required to keep his or her attention on operating the vehicle. The driver can text, watch a movie, do anything a passenger can do as long as the Level 3 artificial intelligence is driving the car. Level 3 cars may inform the driver in certain situations that attention is needed from the driver. Most cars today that are referred to as self-driving fall under the Level 2 category, where the driver is expected to focus on the road at all times, even with self-driving assistance. The driver must tap the steering wheel every 15 seconds, or the self-driving feature shuts off in Level 2 cars.

Level 4 and 5 are future levels of autonomy where not even a steering wheel is needed. These technologies are in development and Ford expects to have a Level 4 or 5 car ready shortly after 2020.

Audi makes about two million cars a year and a profit of a little over four billion Euros. That makes the Audi slightly less profitable than the other German luxury brands Mercedes and BMW, which currently make around eight billion and six billion Euros in profits annually producing a similar number of cars. Audi offers eight sedan models, two sports cars, and four SUV/crossover models.

The company came together in the early twentieth century as four automakers merged together over the course of a decade, roughly between 1910 and 1920. The four original companies are symbolized in the Audi logo by the four intersecting rings. Three of the original

The 2018 Audi A8 is the first ever car available to the general public with Level 3 driving automation.

companies were German and the other was American. World War I flying ace Eddie Rickenbacker founded the American company, called Rickenbacker. Their cars were high quality but very expensive. The company had developed their own V8 engine, which was the thing of value they brought into the group that became known as Audi.

AN AMERICAN HERO

Eddie Rickenbacker, a founder of the Rickenbacker Motor Company, was the most decorated American fighter pilot of World War I, flying a record total of three hundred combat hours, more than any other pilot during the war. That and founding a car company were hardly his only accomplishments though. Before World War I, Rickenbacker raced in the Indianapolis 500 three times, and in later life, he was the CEO of Eastern Airlines. He also authored the Ace Drummond comic strip in the 1930s. Perhaps most impressively, he once survived twenty-eight days at sea after an airplane crash.

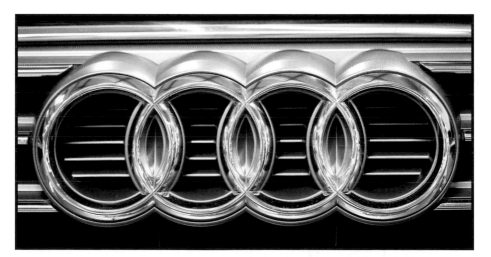

Audi's familiar connected circles logo represents its four original founding companies.

The Porsche 911 is the company's longest continuously produced model and its most familiar.

Porsche

Makers of one of the most recognizable cars on the road, Porsche is known for combining unique body styling with high speed and performance. Porsche's ownership is a little bit of an enigma. Volkswagen Group owns Porsche AG, the manufacturer of Porsche cars, and Volkswagen Group itself is majority owned by the Porsche Automobile Holding Company. The holding company is an investment firm that has ownership stakes in many car companies.

Today's Porsche models include the 911, Boxter, Cayman, Cayenne, Macan, and Panamera. The Cayenne and Macan are Porsche's SUV and crossover models. The 911, Boxter, and Macan are Porsche's sport and roadster models, while the Panamera is their family sedan option.

The 911 is the most well-known Porsche and the oldest in continuous production. Amazingly, for most the car's life, it was an **air-cooled** automobile. Air-cooling was common in small inexpensive cars up until the 1980s. Air-cooling is where the car is engineered to allow natural airflow to cool the engine instead of using a radiator and pump to send liquid coolant around the engine. Many European cars like the original Volkswagen Beetle were air cooled. Porsche's 911 was air cooled until 1998 and was the last production car to be so designed. It was also the only air-cooled production automobile capable of reaching speeds of 200 mph.

911s have not been air cooled for two decades now, and speed still knows no barriers in the 911. The new 911 will be capable of reaching speeds of more than 300 mph.

The Cayenne SUV is known for its several "firsts" and for its recent entry into the Guinness Book of World Records. It was the first Porsche in the twenty-first century to utilize a V8 engine. Its SUV status makes the Cayenne the first Porsche since their tractor line of the 1950s that is meant for off-road use. It's also the first Porsche with four doors, though today's Panamera is a four-door sedan.

In May of 2017, the Cayenne broke the world record for heaviest aircraft pulled by a production automobile. An Air France Airbus weighing 285

The Porsche Cayenne is a powerful vehicle. In 2017 it set the world record for the heaviest aircraft pull by a production vehicle.

tons was pulled forty-two meters. This was accomplished twice using both gasoline and diesel-powered models.

Daimler AG

DAG is the parent company that owns Mercedes-Benz. Its roots go back to the first production automobile and the first cross-country drive. Today they are marketed as cars that first and foremost symbolizes luxury and elegance. Even among their lower-priced vehicles, which start at around $50,000, competitors find it hard to match Mercedes's amenities and style.

The Mercedes line is the only brand under the Daimler name. Mercedes itself has three divisions, Mercedes-Benz, Mercedes AMG, and Maybach. Mercedes-Benz is the most common of the Mercedes line and produces models grouped by class: A, B, C, E, G, and S. AMG stands for Advanced Motors Group, and this division encapsulates their supercar division. AMG cars start around $100,000 to around half a million dollars. Maybach is the advanced supercar, super-luxury model, and a single vehicle can run in the millions of dollars.

Maybach models can cost upwards of one million dollars.

BMW

BMW is a German brand known for its engineering and reliability. The brand came to prominence in American culture in the 1980s as a prestige symbol. A little bit before that, the car first gained popularity in California during the 1950s as an inexpensive and reliable alternative to Detroit automobiles. During this time, independent dealers sold the car. By 1975, BMW had set up a network of dealers in the United States and began marketing itself as the car of the young and successful.

Today, BMW ranks among the top dozen carmakers in the world and has widened its offering to include the Mini and Rolls-Royce. Its model lineup is grouped by series, and opposite to Mercedes, these are labeled by numbers: 1 Series, 2 Series, 3 Series, and so on through the brand new 8 Series that debuted in 2018. The cars get

BWM 7 series models like this Edition 40 Jahre were the company's top of the line until the 8 series was introduced in 2018.

more expensive as the Series number increases. They also make the X Model line that includes SUVs.

Opel

Opel is a German car brand that was a long-time subsidiary of General Motors and in now part of Groupe PSA (Peugeot-Citroen). The maker sells its Opel line in United Kingdom branded as Vauxhall. The company focuses on small- and mid-size cars priced in the moderate range. They are one of Europe's largest makers of family cars.

The company is another in a long line of automobile makers that started out in the bicycle craze of the mid- to late-nineteenth century. They are also among the small group of carmakers around today that made their first car before the beginning of the twentieth century. The first Opel was made in 1899. In 1929, General Motors made their first investment in the company, assuming full control in 1931.

Today, Opel is a mix of their own models and re-branded GM cars from the states. Group PSA's takeover will likely result in a return to all European production, however that may be with a reduced number of available models.

The Opel Cascada convertible is company's most popular native brand. A two-door, front-wheel drive turbo version is sold in the United States as a Buick and in Australia as a Holden model. This model has a 1.6L engine that is capable of 200 hp while a 1.4L family version is available only in Europe.

Opel sells cars in the UK under the Vauxhall marque.

SELECTIVE BOMBING

It's been long rumored that the Allies had orders to avoid bombing Ford or GM (Opel) factories in Germany. Historians debate the accuracy of interpretations of certain documents, but the overall evidence of the results of bombing campaigns show that more GM and Opel factories survived the war than those of Volkswagen, Mercedes, and Audi.

TEXT-DEPENDENT QUESTIONS

1. What do Audi's four rings symbolize?
2. What brands make up Daimler AG?
3. True or False? Opel sells cars under the Buick brand in the United States.

RESEARCH PROJECT

Germany is known in the auto industry for quality precision engineering. Take a look at other German tech products and find three other examples of products that showcase that famous German engineering. Prepare a brief overview of each.

export market
the exchange for commodities conveyed from one country or region to another for purposes of trade

nationalization
occurs when a country's government seizes the assets of corporations or resources without paying for those assets

self-driving
car technology aimed at actively aiding drivers in operating a vehicle on the road in real time or eliminating the need for drivers altogether by using only artificial intelligence to operate the vehicle

CHAPTER 5

United Kingdom

Unfortunately, there isn't much left of the once-high-flying British car manufacturing industry. In fact, there are no completely British-owned carmakers left in existence, though the most popular marques are still made in the United Kingdom. German, French, Chinese, and Indian companies today own these makers.

Bentley

Bentley began life first as a maker of aluminum pistons for Sopwith Camel airplane engines, and then as a racecar maker. It wasn't until after the start of the Great Depression that Bentley went into the luxury business. Bought by Rolls-Royce in the early 1930s, the first luxury Bentley was the Derby "silent sports cars."

The Bentley S came after the original company designs of the 1930s.

The designs of the 1930s gave way to the classic Bentley S and T Series look. These are the cars that look like they continuously give birth to bowler hat-topped British bankers. The birth of the most famous Bentley, the Corniche, almost did not happen at all. By 1970, parent company Rolls-Royce was floundering. This was at the time the Corniche was under development. A company named Vickers purchased Rolls-Royce, keeping it out of liquidation or **nationalization**, and this allowed the Corniche to see the light of day. Vickers itself sold Rolls-Royce to Volkswagen in 1998.

Today, Bentley makes four models, the Mullsane, Flying Spur, Bentayga, and Continental GT (third generation). Any of these will cost between $200,000 and $500,000, depending on model choice and options. The focus of Bentley has always been on luxury, though the new Continental makes inroads into the latest environmentally-friendly features too. The cars are still made in the United Kingdom, in the company's traditional factory in the town of Crewe.

ROLLS-ING IN IT

While Rolls-Royce the carmaker got itself into financial trouble in the early 1970s, leading to its purchase by Vickers, the airplane engine part of Rolls-Royce has been continuously humming along on its own. In weird bit of business magic, Rolls-Royce kept ownership of all its logos, and gets an income stream from licensing the logos back to the carmaker.

MG

Amazingly, this car company still exists. Its origins are in a company called Morris Garages. The MG company was once known for making small and stylish sports cars. While their cars

The initials for British carmaker MG stand for Morris Garages, after William Morris, the employer of the brand's creator, Morris' general manager Cecil Kimber.

Watch a television commercial from the MG Midget from the 1970s.

from this period are still well known in the United Kingdom, the MG line never caught on in the **export market**. Some efforts were made to compete with the now defunct Triumph brand in the US market in the 1970s, but although they were also British made, Triumph sports cars were less expensive to purchase and easier to maintain.

One-time makers of classic British sports cars, MG has been reimagined under Chinese ownership and now offers vehicles like this MG GS.

The company had management problems through most of its history, suffering from having too many chefs in the kitchen, so to speak. Getting passed around from one conglomerate to another and getting nationalized—where the UK government took partial control of the company—led to a lot of indecision within its management.

But even with internal squabbling, MG managed to turn out some pretty cars. The MG Midget is probably the best known in the American market, where it was available for a time in the mid- to late-1970s. Today MG is owned by the Chinese conglomerate, SAIC, which has revamped the line as a mid-sized luxury car. The Chinese-made cars were reintroduced to the British market in 2011.

Jaguar

Jaguar is the most recognizable British automobile. Though the company has been owned by an American company (Ford) and now an Indian company (Tata) for all of the twenty-first century, the brand remains very British. Design and engineering are done at two sites, the Whitley and the Gaydon Engineering Centres. Engines are built at the Wolverhampton plant with body construction and final assembly was done at three additional factories dotted around the United Kingdom.

The design of the current Jaguar F-type convertible shows how modern the brand has become in recent years.

Today Jaguar has three models types, the F-type, the X-type, and the R-type. The F-type is Jaguar's convertible while the X-type represents three sedan models from compact to full-size. The R-type stands for racing. Today's R-type Jaguar has a massive 510 horsepower engine (380 kW) utilizing a supercharged V8.

Land Rover and their luxury sub brand Range Rover are two iconic British brands that today fall under the Jaguar family. The Rover series began life in much the same way as the American Jeep brand. In 1947, the Rover Company was formed to take advantage of post-war materials and the familiarity returning soldiers had with the just-enough-essential-parts concept of the American Jeep. They were able to churn out a simplified and rugged four-wheel drive vehicle for a fairly inexpensive price.

The Land Rover become popular in the 1980s as the brand had found its way into iconic European movies. The vehicle had a kind of counter-culture vibe to it that fit well with the seasoned world-traveler image many wanted to cultivate by the 80s. Today, Land Rover is known for their mid-size Discovery SUV, a far cry from the bare-bones original Land Rovers.

The Range Rover brand currently focuses on high-end SUVs like this compact convertible Evoque model.

Range Rover became the marque's high-end brand after its launch in the 1970s as a more street-friendly version of the Land Rover. Today the brand focuses on high-end sport utility vehicles like the Evoque and Velar.

Late in 2017, Jaguar began testing their first self-driving car. This was the first road test of a **self-driving** car in the United Kingdom. These tests include using two self-driving cars to test various methods of intercar communication to reduce chances of an accident.

Aston Martin

Aston Martin may well be the most British of the British car brands. Famous for being the car brand of choice for fictional British spy James Bond, the company is headquartered in Gaydon, England. Lionel Martin and Robert Bamford founded the company in 1913, but

The Aston Martin DB11 is one of the latest models from the iconic British carmaker.

it was not until after World War I that they were able to get production off the ground. The new company struggled, however, and Bamford left in 1920, four years before it went bankrupt in 1924.

The company, in various forms, produced about seven hundred cars between 1924 and the start of World War II in 1939. It was not until tractor manufacturer David Brown bought the company for a few thousand British pounds in 1947 that Aston Martin made its mark.

The DB (David Brown) series of cars put the company on the map, starting with the DB1 in 1948 through the DB9, which was produced until 2016. Other models include the Vantage, Virage, Volante and Zogato. The latest DB model, the 11, debuted in 2016. A British-Kuwaiti partnership group now owns the company after it spent several years as part of Ford. Its newest model is an update of the Vantage. The 2019 Aston Martin V8 Vantage was available to its first buyers in June 2018. The electric powered RapidE is due in 2019.

 TEXT-DEPENDENT QUESTIONS

1. True or False? Bentley began as a luxury car company.

2. MG is today owned by what company?

3. What American company once owned Jaguar?

 **RESEARCH PROJECT**

Jaguars, Aston Martins, and Bentleys are distinctly British products. Hop online and come up with three other unmistakably British products and explain what makes them so in a short report.

autonomous driving systems
any computer or robotic system other than a human being that can drive a car

conglomerate
a widely diversified corporation

Global Economic Crisis of 2008
a worldwide loss of trillions of dollars triggered by risky lending practices in the United States mortgage and banking industries

ubiquitous
something that is present everywhere

voting share
the right to vote on matters of corporate policy making in a publicly held company as well as on who will compose the members of its board of directors

zero-emissions
substances discharged into the air as fuel exhaust which contain no carbon dioxide

CHAPTER 6

The Rest of the World

A car is a wonderful toy, something that exists for the purpose of filling up a day with fun. In another sense, they are necessary tools, the primary consideration for such things as commutes to work, school, shopping, doctors, and countless other services. They are both **ubiquitous** and useful.

They are pretty difficult to make too.

Making an automobile requires education, skill, and a passion that can overcome huge business difficulties. Think about sourcing or making all of the parts that go into a car. For a small company with limited funds, cars come together by luck, sweat, and magic if they come together at all. The task requires unique individuals. All around the world, the car business has attracted personalities to match the mystery and mechanics of cars.

Australia

Holden

Australia was the only place other than the United States where a true muscle car was designed, built, and sold. The company that made those cars was Holden. They still exist today as an importer and re-brander of vehicles for the Australian market. The government of Australia recently announced a plan to invest $270 million in Holden for development of further car manufacturing in Australia. This is expected to produce the first home-grown Australia cars in two decades. The company manufactured cars for GM through October 2017.

In the early twentieth century, Edward Holden expanded his grandfather's carriage and saddler business by partnering with

A classic Australian purple Holden Torana on display at a car show in Melbourne, Australia. The Holden Torana was one of the many muscle cars of the 1960s and '70s in Australia.

GM. By the 1970s the Holden Monaro, HX, and HQ models rivaled any of Detroit's muscle cars. They are among the most sought-after muscle cars in America even though Holden never sold them in America. The company continued making and designing some models into the 1990s but relied more and more over time on importing existing models from other companies.

AUSSIE, AUSSIE, YANKEE

All great TV cop shows need a car, and Australia's 1970s crime drama series *Homicide* was no different. What was different was the car. For a nationally iconic TV show, the car should have been a Holden. However, disagreements with the company led the show to make a last-minute decision to use a Ford instead of a Holden.

France

Renault-Nissan-Mitsubishi

It's hard to know how to define these three companies. Each is a separate company, that's true, but what is called the Renault-Nissan-Mitsubishi alliance operates with a business model that according to the alliance's Chairman, Carlos Ghosn, has, "engaged in a unique alliance to generate

French carmaker Renault calls the shots in the Renault-Nissan-Mitsubishi alliance.

synergies for all of the companies involved." Forbes called Ghosn "the hardest-working man in the brutally competitive global car business." The Brazilian-born Ghosn is a French citizen who speaks four languages. He is viewed as the savior of Nissan (he was CEO of the company from 2001–2017), and his life story was made into a superhero comic book in Japan.

One in ten cars sold in the world come from this alliance. Renault is historically a French car company, and Nissan and Mitsubishi have origins in Japan. Renault owns 43% of Nissan, which is a full **voting share**, meaning Renault effectively controls the alliance (Ghosn is Renault's CEO). Their unique strategy combines Renault's decades of marketing knowledge about European car buyers, with some of the world's most efficient supply chains.

One of the main goals of this alliance is to bring about full-scale development and production of **zero-emission** vehicles. To that end, the alliance has produced the Nissan Leaf and Renault Zoe cars, which are among the top-selling plug-in electric cars in the world.

The Leaf surpassed the important 300,000-unit milestone in January of 2018. The Renault Kangoo is a zero-emission utility van. Sales of the Kangoo have reached the 25,000-unit mark, making it the top-selling electric utility van in the world.

Groupe PSA

In 2016 the company known as Peugeot-Citroen, combining two of France's oldest car brands became Groupe PSA. The group changed its name after they acquired GM-owned German family carmaker Opel. Other brands under the group are Vauxhall, DS, and Ambassador—a brand originally owned by India's first automobile company, Hindustan.

Peugeot is the oldest continually existing carmaker in the world.

Peugeot is the oldest continually existing company that makes automobiles, though this accounts for only around two-thirds of its history. The company began in 1810 making coffee grinders and by 1830 was a bicycle manufacturer. In 1882 Peugeot became a car company, sort of. At least that's when the company said they were going into the car business. The first Peugeot automobile, which had three wheels and was steam powered, appeared in 1882.

Watch comedian and car-enthusiast Jay Leno explain the unique features of the 1971 Citroen DS in an episode of his series Jay Leno's Garage. He describes it as the most innovative car ever made.

Bugatti

Today's Bugatti revives an elegant name from the past, the name of Italian car designer Ettore Bugatti. The original company was a French-German-Italian outfit that saw its demise after its factory was destroyed in World War II.

The Bugatti that exists in France today is a subsidiary of Volkswagen Group and has produced two of the worlds most renowned supercars, the Chiron and the Veyron.

The Chiron is actually capable of going faster than its electronically limited top speed of 266 mph (420 km/h). The car automatically throttles back at 266 mph (420 km/h) because there are currently no street legal tires capable of handling the cars maximum physical speed of 288 mph (463 km/h). A Bugatti Chiron will set back a buyer a sweet $2.6 million.

The Veyron is the predecessor of the Chiron. At $1.7 million, a Veyron buyer gets what is recognized by the Guinness Book of World Records as the fastest street-legal car in the world, though its official top speed of 267 mph (431 km/h) and other specs are roughly that of the Chiron. The last Veyron was made in 2015.

The Bugatti Chiron, seen here at the 2018 Brussels Motor Show in Belgium, has a top speed of 288 mph (463 km/h).

Italy

Fiat-Chrysler

While it would be fair to say that this is one of the oldest auto companies in the world, it is also one of the newest. Fiat-Chrysler came into existence during the **Global Economic Crisis of 2008**, after two separate car companies on two separate continents (North America and Europe) decided to join forces in order to better weather the crisis.

On the North American side, Chrysler currently maintains only two models under its own brand, the 300 series and the Pacifica minivan. The other primary Chrysler products are the Dodge Charger, ram trucks and the Jeep models.

The Fiat part of the partnership (which has controlling interest in the group) has a long history in Europe and a bumpy history in the United States. The Fiat 500 returned to the United States in 2009 after the merger and is currently one of the most popular compact cars on the market. It's luxury styling is unique among compact cars.

The 500 began sales in the United States in the 1950s, and more models followed. The compact convertible competed with models from MG and Triumph and was popular in the mid-1970s. A sales slide resulting from a reputation for poor workmanship led Fiat to leave the US market in 1983.

The Chrysler Pacifica, like this 2018 hybrid model, is one of the few remaining models bearing the once substantial Chrysler marque.

However, this wasn't Fiat's first departure. Fiat first entered the United States in the early twentieth century, building a plant in New Jersey where they manufactured cars until the outbreak of World War I, when the company first left the United States.

PT LOSER

The Chrysler PT Cruiser was an innovation for Chrysler that came into the world with bang and left after a prolonged whimper. Hailed as a game-changing retro-design innovation, the initial love for the PT Cruiser faded after people bought and drove them. While the car harkened back to 1960s surf-mobiles, the function of car was less than ideal. It broke down a lot, has poor instrumentation, has blind spots and most drivers reported that it was uncomfortable.

Alfa Romeo

Best known for their racing cars, Alfa Romeo produces a wider line of vehicles exclusively for European buyers. Their 147 model is a popular small family car. They also make light utility trucks that are used for, among other things, delivery vans and ambulances.

At the 2018 North American International Auto Show in Detroit, Alfa Romeo showed off its 2018 Alfa Romeo 4C.

The company was founded in 1910 in Milan by Alexandre Darracq, the third successful company founded by the industrious Frenchman with a notorious dislike of driving. The purpose of Alfa Romeo was making a mass-market vehicle. That plan took a turn and Alfa Romeo racing cars became legends throughout the twentieth century. All around the world they are known as the car that wins Grand Prix and endurance races. Around Europe, the Alfa Romeo logo is found on buses, trollies, and family automobiles. Fiat bought the brand in 1986 and has exported the cars to the United States since 2008.

Maserati

One of Italy's oldest automakers, today the company is also part of Fiat but has its own unique history and style. Maserati is named for the four brothers who founded it in 1926. The company continues to make cars today much the same way they always have. Interior styling is a priority for Maserati, with some the finest materials and woods going to the interior of their vehicles.

They make luxury cars that aim for the higher end of the market. The Quattroporte competes with the Mercedes S-Class while the GranTurismo goes after buyers of cars like the Lamborghini Urus, that particular supercar maker's least-expensive model.

The 2018 Maserati Quattroporte targets buyers who might also consider a Mercedes-Benz S-class vehicle.

Ferrari

Most car companies have followed the pattern of making a production car first, then moving on to making racing cars. Ferrari is a company that went the opposite direction. What began as the racecar company that broke all the records, developed into one of the world's first sports car/supercar makers. Enzo Ferrari was a race driver turned entrepreneur known for his fiery personality. He founded his company after leaving Alfa Romeo in 1939.

The first Ferrari saw the race track in 1940 and by the post-World War II era, Grand Prix after Grand Prix was won by a Ferrari. Today, the company still makes top quality racers, along with their current line of eight supercars.

The LaFerrari represents the top end of the Ferrari line. Referred to as hypercars, the LaFerrari and LaFerrari Aperta sport V12 engines with HY-KERs. HY-KER is a system for storing kinetic energy during braking that can be used later in acceleration.

The original LaFerrari came to market in 2013. Only five hundred have been made. 499 of those have been sold, with one remaining to be

The 2018 LaFerrari represents the top of the Ferrari line.

sold at auction at a later date. The Aperta convertible version of the LaFerrari came out in 2016. 210 of these were made, again with one saved to be sold at auction. That auction occurred in 2017 at the famous Sotheby's auction house. That Aperta sold for $10 million. The previous models had a retail price of $3.9 million.

Lamborghini

Though an Italian company through and through, Lamborghini is today a subsidiary of Volkswagen through its own Audi subsidiary. Founded by industrialist Ferruccio Lamborghini in 1963 to compete with Ferrari, the company currently has three models, two sports cars, and an SUV. The logo for the brand comes from Lamborghini's love of bullfighting.

The Aventador and Huracan are the sports car models, and the Urus is their SUV. The Urus, introduced in 2018, is one the lightest SUVs due to its use of carbon-poly fiber in the construction of its body. It has a V8 engine and can reach a top speed of 190 mph (305 km/h). The name comes from the ancestor of today's modern cow, which was much larger and meaner than today's docile animals.

The 2018 Lamborghini Aventador was on display at the 2017 Frankfurt IAA Motor Show in Germany.

The ride share application company Uber has been using Volvos to test self-driving technology in San Francisco.

The Aventador and the Huracan compete with Ferrari, Bugatti, and other supercar brands. A V10 engine, with a V12 option, powers both cars. Standard Aventadors reach top speeds of 217 mph (350 km/h). By comparison, the Huracan has a top speed of 212 mph (341 km/h). The name comes from the Mayan god of fire. *Top Gear* named the car The Supercar of the Year 2014.

Sweden

Volvo

Volvo is another old-school car company that is now in the hands of a Chinese **conglomerate**. In the coming years, it may become the first major car company of the twentieth century to end production of internal combustion-only vehicles. All vehicles planned for the years ahead have hybrid or electric power systems. Uber, the multinational car and driver-for-hire app that exploded onto the scene in 2012 and which secured $2 billion in funding in 2015 has pre-ordered twenty-four thousand Volvo cars that will be able to accept **autonomous driving systems**.

Volvo began as a Swedish company in 1927, an offshoot of a large machining company. The guiding principle of the company has always been that Volvo should manufacture the safest cars on the road. They have won many awards and high marks in reviews for their dedication and innovations in car safety.

South Korea
Hyundai Motor Group

Headquartered in Seoul, this company cranks out nearly five million cars a year. It has a major manufacturing facility in Ulsan, South Korea, but Hyundai builds cars in more than fifteen countries all over the world. The company sells cars in 193 countries.

Its main brand is Hyundai, the marque under which you will find such popular models as the Sonata, Santa Fe, and Tucson.

The Santa Fe is a top-selling Hyundai model in many countries around the world.

Founded in 1967 by entrepreneur Chung Ju-yung, a North Korean native who anticipated the need for infrastructure once South Korea was liberated from Japan after World War II. He made a fortune in construction and shipbuilding after the Korean War and was just as successful with car making.

Hyundai's first success was the Pony, the company's first mass-produced car, which sold extremely well in Europe, South America, and Canada.

Hyundai also owns a third of Kia Motors another South Korean carmaker that makes three million vehicles a year. In America, Kia is well known for the Soul, Sorento, and Sportage models.

TEXT-DEPENDENT QUESTIONS

1. What country other than the United States made home-grown muscle cars?

2. What was it about the body of the Puma car that made it different?

3. True or False? Saturn was a subsidiary of GM.

RESEARCH PROJECT

Virtual Car Restoration. Go on the Internet and pick a make and model of a car made by one of these defunct companies. Make a list of original parts that you can find (using eBay or any number of parts websites) for your chosen vehicle. Suggested parts include carburetor, radiator, pumps, ignition systems, brake parts, and exhaust parts.

Series Glossary of Terms

Aerodynamic Drag
Drag produced by a moving object as it displaces the air in its path. Aerodynamic drag is a force usually measured in pounds; it increases in proportion to the object's frontal area, its drag coefficient, and the square of its speed.

Ball Joint
A flexible joint consisting of a ball in a socket, used primarily in front suspensions because it can accommodate a wide range of angular motion.

Camshaft
A shaft fitted with several cams, whose lobes push on valve lifters to convert rotary motion into linear motion. One or more camshafts regulate the opening and closing of the valves in all piston engines.

Carbon Fiber
Threadlike strands of pure carbon that are extremely strong in tension (that is, when pulled) and are reasonably flexible. Carbon fiber can be bound in a matrix of plastic resin by heat, vacuum, or pressure to form a composite that is strong and light—and very expensive.

Chassis
A general term that refers to all of the mechanical parts of a car attached to a structural frame. In cars with unitized construction, the chassis comprises everything but the body of the car.

Cylinder
The round, straight-sided cavity in which the pistons move up and down. Typically made of cast iron and formed as a part of the block.

Differential
A special gearbox designed so that the torque fed into it is split and delivered to two outputs that can turn at different speeds. Differentials within axles are designed to split torque evenly; however, when used between the front and rear axles in four-wheel-drive systems (a center differential), they can be designed to apportion torque unevenly.

Drivetrain
All of a car's components that create power and transmit it to the wheels; i.e. the engine, the transmission, the differential(s), the hubs, and any interconnecting shafts.

Fuel Injection
Any system that meters fuel to an engine by measuring its needs and then regulating the fuel flow, by electronic or mechanical means, through a pump and injectors. Throttle-body injection locates the injector(s) centrally in the throttle-body housing, while port injection allocates at least one injector for each cylinder near its intake port.

Horsepower
The common unit of measurement of an engine's power. One horsepower equals 550 foot-pounds per second, the power needed to lift 550 pounds one foot off the ground in one second: or one pound 550 feet up in the same time.

Intake Manifold
The network of passages that direct air or air-fuel mixture from the throttle body to the intake ports in the cylinder head. The flow typically proceeds from the throttle body into a chamber called the plenum, which in turn feeds individual tubes, called runners, leading to each intake port. Engine breathing is enhanced if the intake manifold is configured to optimize the pressure pulses in the intake system.

Overdrive

Any gearset in which the output shaft turns faster than the input shaft. Overdrive gears are used in most modern transmissions because they reduce engine rpm and improve fuel economy.

Overhead Cam

The type of valvetrain arrangement in which the engine's camshaft(s) is in its cylinder head(s). When the camshaft(s) is placed close to the valves, the valvetrain components can be stiffer and lighter, allowing the valves to open and close more rapidly and the engine to run at higher rpm. In a single-overhead-cam (SOHC) layout, one camshaft actuates all of the valves in a cylinder head. In a double-overhead-camshaft (DOHC) layout, one camshaft actuates the intake valves, and one camshaft operates the exhaust valves.

Powertrain

An engine and transmission combination.

Rack-and-Pinion

A steering mechanism that consists of a gear in mesh with a toothed bar, called a ""rack."" The ends of the rack are linked to the steered wheels with tie rods. When the steering shaft rotates the gear, it moves the rack from side to side: turning the wheels.

Sedan

As used by *Car and Driver*, the term "sedan" refers to a fixed-roof car with at least four doors or any fixed-roof two-door car with at least 33 cubic feet of rear interior volume, according to measurements based on SAE standard J1100.

Shock Absorber

A device that converts motion into heat, usually by forcing oil through small internal passages in a tubular housing. Used primarily to dampen suspension oscillations, shock absorbers respond to motion.

Spoiler

An aerodynamic device that changes the direction of airflow in order to reduce lift or aerodynamic drag and/or improve engine cooling.

Supercharger

An air compressor used to force more air into an engine than it can inhale on its own. The term is frequently applied only to mechanically driven compressors, but it actually encompasses all varieties of compressors.

Turbocharger

A supercharger powered by an exhaust-driven turbine. Turbochargers always use centrifugal-flow compressors, which operate efficiently at the high rotational speeds produced by the exhaust turbine.

Source: caranddriver.com

FURTHER READING

Davis, Michael W. R., and James K. Wagner. *Ford Dynasty: A Photographic History*. Mount Pleasant: Arcadia Publishing, 2002.

Rothfeder, Jeffrey. *Driving Honda: Inside the World's Most Innovative Car Company*. New York City: Portfolio, 2014.

Naldrett, Alan. *Lost Car Companies of Detroit.* Stroud: The History Press, 2016.

Goldstone, Lawrence. *Drive!: Henry Ford, George Selden, and the Race to Invent the Auto Age.* New York City: Ballantine, 2016.

INTERNET RESOURCES

www.thehenryford.org/ - The website of The Henry Ford museum. They have an extensive online collection of stories and videos about some of the twenty-six million artifacts in their collection.

corporate.ford.com/history.html - The history section of the Ford website has an interactive timeline and lot of additional information about the history of the company.

www.toyota.co.jp/Museum/english/ - The website for the Toyota museum in Japan. Many of the online exhibits are available in both Japanese and English.

dodgemotorcar.com/ - The independent website with lots of images and stories about the history of Dodge cars.

www.automuseum.org/ - The website for the National Auto Museum in Reno, NV.

EDUCATIONAL VIDEOS:

Chapter 1:
http://x-qr.net/1Dnv

Chapter 2:
http://x-qr.net/1HiC

Chapter 3:
http://x-qr.net/1Ecp

Chapter 4:
http://x-qr.net/1Eda

Chapter 5:
http://x-qr.net/1DfV

Chapter 6:
http://x-qr.net/1Etn

PHOTO CREDITS:

INDEX

INDEX

INDEX

AUTHOR'S BIOGRAPHY

Norm Geddis lives in Southern California where he works as a writer, video editor, and collectibles expert. He once spent two years cataloging and appraising over one million old movie props. He is currently restoring film and video content from the 1950's DuMont Television Network for the Days of DuMont channel on Roku.